BLOBFISH

Discovering the World's Perfectly Pink Animals

by **JESS KEATING**

with illustrations by **DAVID DeGRAND**

Alfred A. Knopf

Think you know

PINK?

Think again . . .

Pink is for BLOBFISH.

Bizarre **BLOBFISH** are made of a **gelatinous** goo, which is less dense than water. This allows them to lazily drift through the ocean like bloated pink balloons. Blobfish don't hunt for food. Instead, when something edible floats by, they simply open their mouths and gulp it down.

Pretty in Pink?

The blobfish was recently voted the ugliest animal in the world in a poll taken by the Ugly Animal Preservation Society. Luckily, blobfish don't use mirrors, so they aren't bothered by their less-than-cute faces. As if this wasn't bad enough, another name for the blobfish is "fathead sculpin." These fish can't catch a break!

Name: Blobfish

Species name: *Psychrolutes marcidus*

Size: Up to 12 inches (30 centimeters) from nose to tail

Diet: Almost anything edible that floats by, including snails, worms, crustaceans, and other slow-moving animals

Habitat: The deep waters surrounding Australia and New Zealand, where few animals can survive

Predators and threats: Blobfish have no known predators and are inedible to humans, yet many scientists believe they may face extinction soon, as they are often caught in fishermen's nets by accident.

Pink is for PINKTOE TARANTULAS.

It is very easy to spot mysterious Antilles **PINKTOE TARANTULAS** in pet stores, but much harder to find them in the wild. At night, they scurry out of their funnel webs high in the trees to search for food.

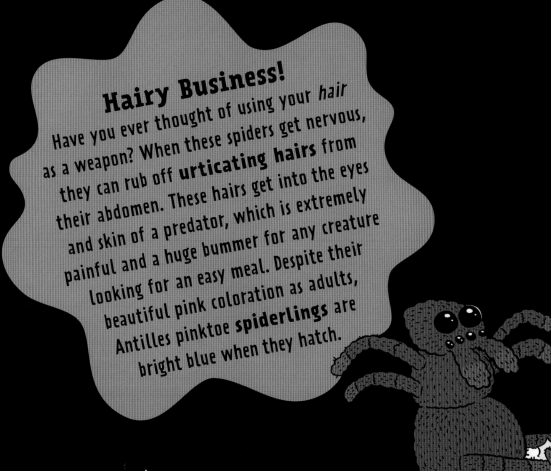

Hairy Business!

Have you ever thought of using your *hair* as a weapon? When these spiders get nervous, they can rub off **urticating hairs** from their abdomen. These hairs get into the eyes and skin of a predator, which is extremely painful and a huge bummer for any creature looking for an easy meal. Despite their beautiful pink coloration as adults, Antilles pinktoe **spiderlings** are bright blue when they hatch.

Name: Antilles pinktoe tarantula

Species name: *Avicularia versicolor*

Size: 4–6 inches (10.2–15.2 centimeters)

Diet: Insects, worms, and small lizards

Habitat: The rain forests of Martinique and Guadeloupe, off the northern coast of South America

Predators and threats: These creatures need trees to survive and build their webs, so **deforestation** may eventually pose a threat to them.

Pink is for ORCHID MANTISES.

With flattened, petal-like arms that stand out against green leaves, **ORCHID MANTISES** look like harmless, beautiful flowers. But these pretenders have strong arms and big appetites, patiently waiting to snatch up any insect that comes too close.

Name: Orchid mantis

Species name: *Hymenopus coronatus*

Size: 0.5–6 inches (1.3–15.2 centimeters)

Diet: Insects, like crickets and flies, as well as some small lizards

Habitat: The rain forests of Indonesia and Malaysia

Predators and threats: Orchid mantises live in areas with many white and pink flowers. The same coloration that lures prey to them also works as **camouflage** against would-be predators, such as birds, toads, rodents, bats, and lizards. Like other rain forest creatures, their gravest threat stems from habitat loss due to human development.

Made Ya Look!

Sometimes nature can be tricky. Scientists wanted to know if the insects that landed on orchid mantises were really fooled into thinking they were flowers. They came up with an experiment where they gave insects a choice: they could land on an orchid mantis or on a *real* Malaysian flower. And voilà! It turned out that the insects picked mantises more often than actual flowers!

Pink is for PYGMY SEAHORSES.

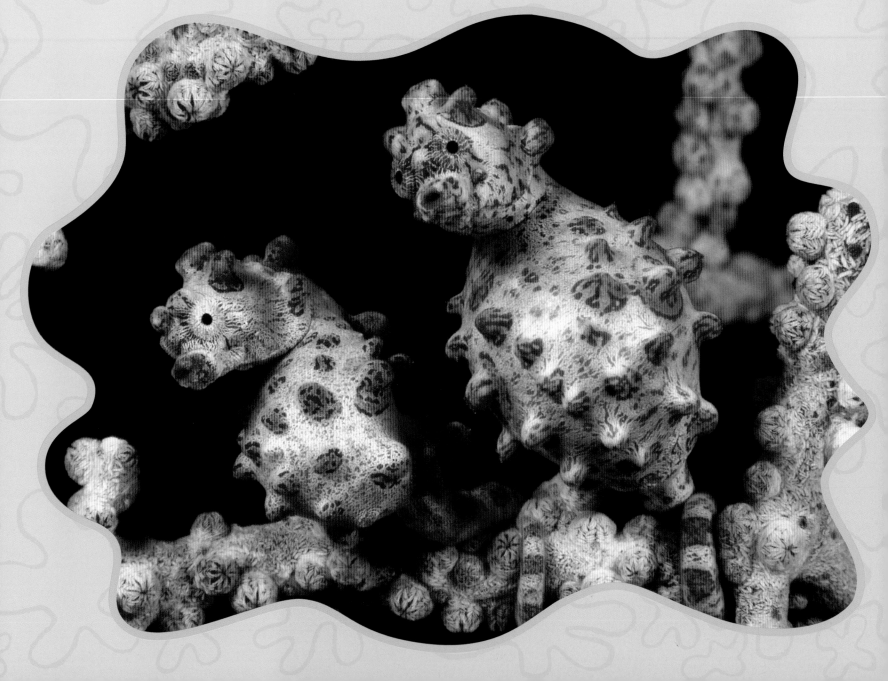

PYGMY SEAHORSES hide out in plain sight, nestled amongst the pink coral of the ocean floor. They are extremely fragile, so it's important for scuba divers to be careful around them. Even the bright flash of a camera can disturb them.

#1 Dad!

In most animal species, it is usually the female who becomes pregnant and gives birth. But seahorses don't care about tradition. Instead, male seahorses become pregnant and carry the eggs in a pouch on their bellies until they hatch. If that isn't enough to earn them the Dad of the Year Award, they also keep the eggs clean and protect them from predators.

#1 DAD!

Name: Barbigant's pygmy seahorse

Species name: *Hippocampus barbiganti*

Size: Up to 1.1 inches (27 millimeters)

Diet: Tiny crustaceans, such as brine shrimp

Habitat: The waters surrounding Indonesia, Papua New Guinea, Philippines, Malaysia, Japan, and northern Australia

Predators and threats: Many of the world's seahorse populations are decreasing. In some countries, seahorses are believed to have medicinal properties. Because of this, millions of them are caught every year. Seahorses are also threatened by loss of habitat, as their favorite sea grasses, reefs, and mangroves are declining worldwide.

Pink is for ROSEATE SPOONBILLS.

Not all pink animals are born pink. When baby **SPOONBILLS** hatch, they are chubby and covered in downy white feathers. As they grow up, their feathers turn various shades of pink because of **pigments** in the shrimp they eat.

Want a Feather in Your Cap?

In the past, women used to wear hats decorated with vibrant spoonbill feathers. Fans made of spoonbill wings were also very popular. Because of aggressive "plume hunters," the roseate spoonbill was once nearly extinct. By 1940, there were only about thirty breeding pairs left in a Florida flock that previously contained thousands. Today, thanks to conservation efforts, their numbers have rebounded.

Name: Roseate spoonbill

Species name: *Platalea ajaja*

Size: Roughly 28–34 inches tall (71.1–86.4 centimeters), with a wingspan of 4 feet 4 inches (1.3 meters)

Diet: Aquatic invertebrates, fish, amphibians, and plants

Habitat: Marshes, ponds, swamps, mangroves, and rivers are spoonbill breeding grounds. They are found along the Gulf Coast of the United States and in South America, Central America, and the West Indies.

Predators and threats: Entire colonies have been known to leave their homes because of coastal development and pollution, and some flocks now live in wildlife refuges, where conservationists monitor their numbers. Raccoons, coyotes, and hawks also prey on spoonbill eggs and young.

Pink is for AMAZON RIVER DOLPHINS.

AMAZON RIVER DOLPHINS are very intelligent, and they have extremely complex ways of hunting. Several dolphins work together as a group to drive fish near the shore, like a pack of dogs herding sheep. With the fish stranded close to land, the dolphins can enjoy a fishy feast together.

A Different Dolphin!

Unlike dolphins from the open ocean, Amazon river dolphins have flexible necks. They sweep their snouts through the watery vegetation, flushing prey from their hiding places. A new species of dolphin, the Araguaian river dolphin, was just discovered in 2014. It was the first new river dolphin species found in almost a century! River dolphins are incredibly rare, so finding a new species is a huge feat!

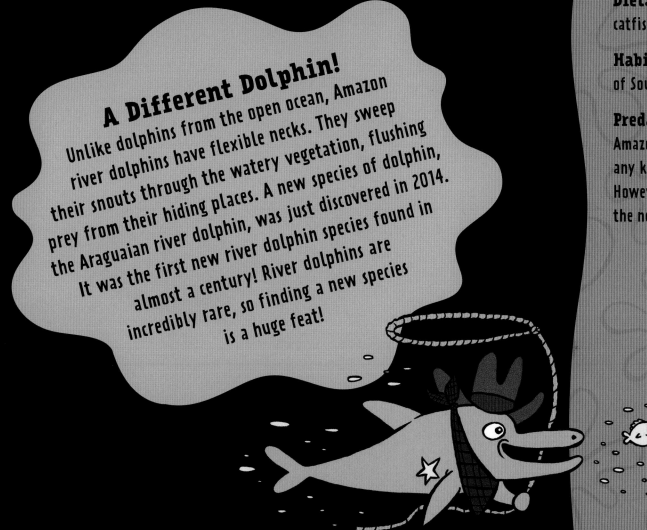

Name: Amazon river dolphin

Species name: *Inia geoffrensis*

Size: Ranges from 6–9 feet (1.8–2.7 meters)

Diet: Bottom-dwelling fish, catfish, piranhas, and crustaceans

Habitat: The freshwater rivers of South America

Predators and threats: Amazon river dolphins don't have any known natural predators. However, they are often caught in the nets of local fishermen.

Pink is for PINK FAIRY ARMADILLOS.

You won't find these creatures in any fairy tale! PINK FAIRY ARMADILLOS are very real, and very hard to find. They have flexible, rosy pink shells on their backs, and enormous claws that they use to burrow through the dirt. They are only seen by humans when they emerge aboveground. This happens so rarely that some armadillo researchers *never* see them in the wild!

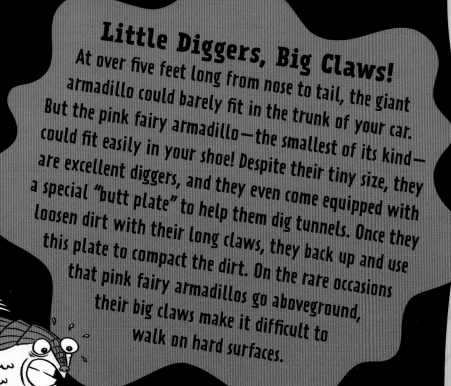

Little Diggers, Big Claws!

At over five feet long from nose to tail, the giant armadillo could barely fit in the trunk of your car. But the pink fairy armadillo—the smallest of its kind—could fit easily in your shoe! Despite their tiny size, they are excellent diggers, and they even come equipped with a special "butt plate" to help them dig tunnels. Once they loosen dirt with their long claws, they back up and use this plate to compact the dirt. On the rare occasions that pink fairy armadillos go aboveground, their big claws make it difficult to walk on hard surfaces.

Name: Pink fairy armadillo

Species name: *Chlamyphorus truncatus*

Size: 4 inches (10.2 centimeters)

Diet: Worms, as well as ants and other small insects

Habitat: The sandy plains and scrubby grasslands of southern South America

Predators and threats: Pink fairy armadillos depend on the soil to survive. Because of this, farmers working the land can accidentally force them out of their homes. Herds of cattle walking on the dirt can compress the soil, making it difficult for them to burrow, and they are also hunted by dogs, cats, coyotes, and wild boars.

Pink is for SOUTHERN BLIND SNAKES.

Although this creature looks like an earthworm, you won't find it in your backyard! Unless your backyard is in Australia, that is. **SOUTHERN BLIND SNAKES** use their thick skulls and hard scales to burrow deep into the earth, slithering through the soil to find food.

Hide and Seek!

Some animals are so good at hiding, they aren't seen for decades, no matter how hard scientists look. In 1905, a new species of blind snake was discovered in Madagascar. It would be one hundred years before scientists found another of its kind! Despite their name, blind snakes aren't actually blind, but they are **negatively phototaxic**. This is a fancy way of saying they avoid light, which might be why they're such great hiders.

Name: Southern blind snake

Species name: *Ramphotyphlops australis*

Size: Up to 18 inches (46 centimeters)

Diet: Larvae and eggs of termites and ants

Habitat: The forests and scrublands of Western Australia

Predators and threats: Like many Australian species, blind snakes are threatened by habitat loss and wildfires. Very little is known about their predators, but it is possible that **introduced species** hunt these snakes.

Pink is for HOPKINS' ROSE NUDIBRANCHS.

HOPKINS' ROSE NUDIBRANCH is one of the pinkest creatures in the ocean. It may look like it's made entirely of bubble gum, but don't let that fool you. Hopkins' rose isn't gum *or* a rose— it's really a sea snail without the shell. Instead, it has several finger-like projections that wave freely in the ocean currents.

Plenty of Nudibranchs in the Sea!

Like many species of snails, nudibranchs are **hermaphroditic**. This means they have both male *and* female organs and can mate with any mature nudibranch of their species. Doubling your dating pool comes in handy when you live in a vast ocean, where fellow nudibranchs are hard to find!

Name: Hopkins' rose nudibranch

Species name: *Okenia rosacea*

Size: Approximately 0.8–1.2 inches in length (20–30 millimeters)

Diet: Invertebrate animals, specifically colonies of moss animals, called **bryozoans**, that live on rocks in the water

Habitat: The rocky shores and tide pools on the west coast of North America, from southern Oregon to Baja California

Predators and threats: Usually, nudibranchs are only eaten by other nudibranchs. Most would-be predators avoid them because of their bitter taste. But the tide pools where they live are also very popular with human visitors. Because of this, nudibranchs and other nearby species can be stepped on or even captured in their natural environments.

Pink is for NAKED MOLE RATS.

NAKED MOLE RATS are **eusocial** rodents. This means that they work as a team to survive, with some mole rats digging tunnels and finding food while others defend against attacks or take care of young. Naked mole rats might also one day save human lives. Doctors and medical scientists have recently discovered the rodent's ability to stay cancer-free, which could lead to important advances in the treatment of cancer patients. Not bad for a creature that looks like a pink potato with teeth!

Hail to the Queen!

Naked mole rat colonies are led by a single queen. She is the only one that has babies, while other mole rats work hard to keep the colony safe and well-fed. Naked mole rats are also talented architects, building elaborate homes with special chambers, including a toilet, a nursery, and even a pantry for storing food! There are no closets, though— who needs clothes when you were born to be naked?

Name: Naked mole rat

Species name: *Heterocephalus glaber*

Size: 3–4 inches (7.6–10.2 centimeters), with a tail up to 3 inches long (7.6 centimeters)

Diet: Roots and tubers; they also eat their own poop, which helps them get more nutrients from their food

Habitat: The sandy soil of Kenya, Somalia, and Ethiopia, in East Africa

Predators and threats: Birds and snakes will attempt to eat naked mole rats if they catch a glimpse of them. However, these creatures will often call out a chirping or squeaking alarm as soon as a predator is spotted, so they are very tough to surprise!

Pink is for PINK SEA STARS.

PINK SEA STARS have hundreds of sticky **tube feet** on their arms, allowing them to cling to rocks on the ocean floor while they search for prey. They also have another trick up their sleeve (er . . . *arm*) when it comes to feeding. If a sea star comes across prey that is too big to fit *in* its mouth, it will stick its stomach *out* through its mouth, wrap it around its meal, digest it, and then draw the goopy, digested mess back into its body. Some might think this is gross, but seasoned animal explorers know the truth: it's seriously cool.

The World's Best Party Trick!

If you've ever been to the beach, you might have seen sea stars on the rocks. Although these can be hard and brittle when they're dead, living sea stars are soft and flabby. They may look defenseless, but if a predator attacks, they can shed an arm, leaving it behind while they make their escape. Don't feel too bad for them, though—whenever they lose an arm, they just grow it back!

Name: Pink sea star

Species name: *Pisaster brevispinus*

Size: Up to a diameter of 2 feet (60 centimeters)

Diet: Clams, snails, sand dollars, barnacles; they may also scavenge dead fish or squid

Habitat: In the sandy or muddy waters from Alaska to California

Predators and threats: Because of their tough skeletons, sea stars have few natural predators as adults. However, sometimes sea stars do try to eat each other! Along with their hard armor, some sea stars contain chemicals called **saponins**. These chemicals taste terrible, making them a great defense against would-be predators.

Pink is for HIPPOPOTAMUSES.

HIPPOPOTAMUSES spend long days in some of the hottest parts of the world. To protect themselves from sunburn, hippos ooze a thick pink oil all over their skin. This pink "sweat" acts like an antibiotic sunscreen, so hippos can stay out in the sun all day without getting burned.

Sink or Swim!

Hippos spend up to sixteen hours a day submerged in the water to keep cool. They can close their nostrils and ears and hold their breath for five minutes as they trot along the river bottom. But water-loving hippos also have a well-kept secret. Despite their **amphibious** lifestyle, they can't actually swim—they're even too dense to float! Instead, they gracefully walk through the water, with their toes lightly bouncing off the bottom of the riverbed.

Name: Hippopotamus

Species name: *Hippopotamus amphibius*

Size: 9–14 feet (2.8–4.2 meters), with a tail up to 13.7–19.7 inches (30–50 centimeters)

Diet: Grasses and fruit

Habitat: Near rivers, lakes, and swamps of sub-Saharan Africa

Predators and threats: Despite their lumbering, chubby appearance, hippos are one of the most dangerous animals in Africa. In fact, hippos kill more people than any other large animal in Africa, including lions and crocodiles. Their enormous size and long, sharp teeth make them deadly to predators like lions, but they still have to watch out for each other. Male hippos often fight for territory, which can cause serious injury or even death.

Pink is for PINK SLUGS.

Beneath the decaying twigs and leaf litter of the misty forest lies a slimy secret. **PINK SLUGS** produce two types of **mucus**. One type of "slime" prevents the slug from slipping on surfaces. The second type is excreted all over the slug's body, protecting it from predators. It is very hard to pick up a slimy slug, because they are so slippery.

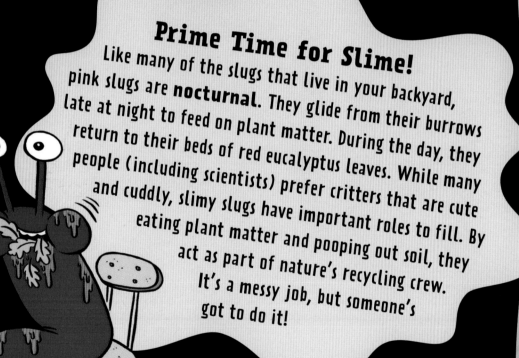

Prime Time for Slime!

Like many of the slugs that live in your backyard, pink slugs are **nocturnal**. They glide from their burrows late at night to feed on plant matter. During the day, they return to their beds of red eucalyptus leaves. While many people (including scientists) prefer critters that are cute and cuddly, slimy slugs have important roles to fill. By eating plant matter and pooping out soil, they act as part of nature's recycling crew. It's a messy job, but someone's got to do it!

Name: Pink slug

Species name: *Triboniophorus aff. graeffei*

Size: Up to 8 inches (20.3 centimeters)

Diet: Mold, moss, and algae

Habitat: The forests of Mount Kaputar, Australia

Predators and threats: Along with other animals that live in sensitive environments, pink slugs are threatened by **climate change**. This occurs when gases in our atmosphere trap the sun's heat, warming up the planet. Even a temperature increase of one or two degrees could destroy the plants and animals of this unique area.

Pink is for PINK LAND IGUANAS.

PINK LAND IGUANAS are large reptiles that live on a single isolated volcano on one small island in the Galápagos, surviving off cactus pads, fallen fruit, and shrubs. Scientists used to think they were the same as other yellow land iguanas on the island, but in 2009, they took a closer look. Not only were pink iguanas a species of their own, but they branched off from the yellow iguanas 5.7 million years ago! It is thought that fewer than one hundred of these **elusive** animals still exist.

Return of the Reptiles!

Charles Darwin, a famous **naturalist**, first discovered land iguanas in the Galápagos in 1835. Back then, the Galápagos were full of these unique reptiles. In 1975, land iguanas almost went **extinct** after large packs of wild dogs preyed on them. To help preserve the species, iguanas were bred in captivity and introduced back to the wild once the dogs were removed. By 2008, the breeding program was a success, and today their numbers are growing!

Name: Pink land iguana

Species name: *Conolophus marthae*

Size: Roughly 18.5 inches (47 centimeters), with 24-inch tails (61 centimeters)

Diet: Mostly plants, but may also eat insects and **carrion**

Habitat: Wolf Volcano of northern Isla Isabela, in the Galápagos Islands

Predators and threats: Up until they are a year old, young iguanas are easy prey for hawks, herons, and snakes. When they are older, introduced species such as cats and dogs are capable of hunting them.

Pink is for DRAGON MILLIPEDES.

Some insects wear pink to blend in. But the **DRAGON MILLIPEDE** wants to stand out. By sporting hot pink, this millipede sends a message. "Stay away! I'm dangerous!" If a predator tries to take a bite, dragon millipedes can secrete hydrogen cyanide—a toxic chemical—from their bodies.

Trouble Ahead!

These millipedes aren't the only animals that use vivid colors to warn predators. This is called **aposematic coloration**. Poison dart frogs are brightly colored to showcase their toxins, and coral snakes are ringed with yellow and red to flaunt their deadly venom. After a mouthful of bitter toxin or a nasty bite, it doesn't take long for predators to learn to stay away from brightly colored animals! But dragon millipedes aren't all bad news—the hydrogen cyanide in their bodies also makes them smell like almonds!

BACK OFF!

Name: Dragon millipede

Species name: *Desmoxytes purpurosea*

Size: Up to 1.2 inches (30 millimeters)

Diet: Decaying leaves and plant material

Habitat: Southeast Asia, from southeastern China to Vietnam, Thailand, and Myanmar

Predators and threats: Dragon millipedes survive on leaf litter, so they are very sensitive to changes in the soil.

Pink is for RED UAKARIS.

With bright pink faces that stand out against the leaves, **RED UAKARIS** are always on the move, leaping and swinging from tree to tree. You aren't supposed to judge a book by its cover, but you can judge a uakari by its face: the healthier the uakari is, the brighter his face will be. Uakaris with the brightest, pinkest faces are the most attractive to potential mates.

BAM!

Treetop Troopers and Poopers!

Red uakaris are small South American **primates** that live in large groups called troops. One troop can have up to one hundred animals, and as they travel through the treetops, they make the rain forest healthier. Every time uakaris eat fruit, they poop out the seeds, spreading them all around the forest so new trees can grow. Who knew poop was so important? They also knock fruit to the ground when they forage, which feeds other hungry animals below.

Name: Red uakari

Species name: *Cacajao calvus rubicundus*

Size: 15–22.5 inches (38–57 centimeters)

Diet: Fruits, seeds, roots, and the occasional insect

Habitat: The forests of the Amazon River Basin, in Peru and Brazil

Predators and threats: Like many other animals in the trees, uakaris are always on the watch for birds of prey looking for an easy meal. Uakaris also depend on the water in the Amazon river systems to survive, so any pollution in these areas can hurt them. Sadly, these animals are sometimes illegally sold as pets and hunted for their meat.

Pink is for HAIRY SQUAT LOBSTERS.

Talk about a bad hair day! HAIRY SQUAT LOBSTERS' bright pink bodies are covered with purple spots and yellow hairs. Have you ever seen someone with food caught in his mustache? Hairy squat lobsters use the delicate hairs on their body to trap microscopic algae, **plankton**, and bits of fish poop. By "combing" through its food-filled hairs, the hairy squat lobster has an easy meal on the go.

What's in a Name?

Despite its name, the hairy squat lobster isn't a lobster at all; it's actually more closely related to the hermit crab. It can be very hard to see these tiny creatures, as they are well camouflaged to match the barrel sponges they call home. They might not know it, but hairy squat lobsters have one of the oldest homes in the reef! Barrel sponges (often called the "redwoods of the reef") can live for two thousand years, and they provide excellent living quarters for hundreds of animals.

Name: Hairy squat lobster

Species name: *Lauriea siagiani*

Size: Roughly 0.5 inch (13 millimeters)

Diet: Algae, plankton, and fish poop

Habitat: The coral reefs in the southwestern Pacific Ocean, near Indonesia

Predators and threats: It is difficult to fish for one species without accidentally hurting others nearby. Unregulated fishing threatens the Indonesian coral reefs, which are home to many animals, including the hairy squat lobster.

Pink is everywhere!

There's a whole world of colorful creatures out there,
and scientists have discovered only a fraction of them.
Maybe the next big discovery will be yours!

- Amazon river dolphin
- Antilles pinktoe tarantula
- Barbigant's pygmy seahorse
- Blobfish
- Dragon millipede
- Hairy squat lobster
- Hippopotamus
- Hopkins' rose nudibranch
- Naked mole rat
- Orchid mantis
- Pink fairy armadillo
- Pink land iguana
- Pink sea star
- Pink slug
- Red uakari
- Roseate spoonbill
- Southern blind snake

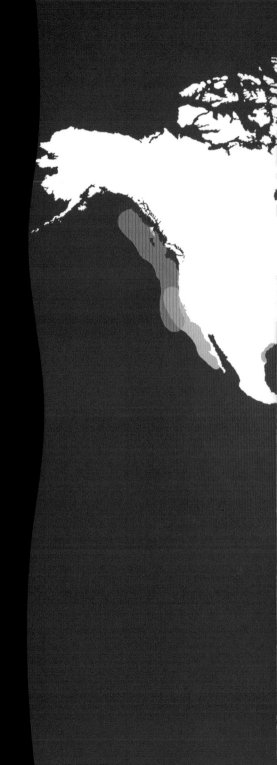

Say What?! A Glossary of Useful Words

Some of the words in the text are in **bold**. If you didn't understand them,
you can use the list below to learn the definition for new terms.

- **Amphibious:** suited to living in both land and water
- **Aposematic coloring:** recognizable colors or markings that serve to warn off predators
- **Bryozoans:** aquatic invertebrates, also called moss animals, that live in colonies attached to rocks or seaweed
- **Camouflage:** hiding from predators, often by blending in with the surroundings
- **Carrion:** dead bodies of animals
- **Climate change:** when the temperatures of the Earth's atmosphere and oceans heat up, affecting animals, plants, and humans
- **Deforestation:** the process of clearing forests, by logging or burning trees
- **Elusive:** difficult to find or see
- **Eusocial:** describing a community of highly organized animals with division of labor and cooperative raising of babies
- **Extinct:** no longer existing in the world
- **Gelatinous:** having a jelly-like consistency
- **Hermaphrodite:** an organism with both male and female reproductive organs
- **Introduced species:** species that are not originally from a given area, but are brought there by humans
- **Mucus:** a slippery fluid secreted by some animals
- **Naturalist:** a scientist who studies the natural history of plants and animals, usually by observing them in their native habitats
- **Negative phototaxis:** when an organism moves away from a source of light
- **Nocturnal:** active at night
- **Pigment:** the natural coloring of an animal or plant
- **Plankton:** microscopic organisms that drift through the sea or fresh water
- **Primate:** a member of the group of animals that includes monkeys, apes, and human beings
- **Saponins:** unpleasant-tasting chemicals found in some sea stars (they are also found in some plants)
- **Spiderling:** a baby spider
- **Tube feet:** small, tubular projections found on the underside of sea stars
- **Urticating hairs:** irritating bristles, used to defend against predators

I Want to Know More!

Scientists are constantly discovering new information about animals. And sometimes what we *think* we know ends up changing because of new research and new discoveries. If you would like to learn more about any of the animals in this book, your local librarian can help you find some great, up-to-date resources to explore. This list can get you started!

Online Resources:

- National Geographic Kids: kids.nationalgeographic.com
- ARKive: arkive.org
- National Audubon Society: web4.audubon.org/educate/kids
- The Keating Creature Collection: jesskeating.com/keatingcreature

Magazines:

- *Ranger Rick* and *Ranger Rick Jr.*: nwf.org/Kids/Ranger-Rick.aspx
- Zoobooks: zoobooks.com

Books:

- *The Animal Book*, by Steve Jenkins
- *National Geographic Animal Encyclopedia*, by Lucy Spelman

When I Grow Up . . .

The world is full of animals for you to discover, and there are many different types of scientists who study them. What creatures amaze you the most?

I want to learn about **insects**. You can be an **entomologist**.

I want to learn about **marine animals**. You can be a **marine biologist**.

I want to learn about **reptiles**. You can be a **herpetologist**.

I want to learn about **birds**. You can be an **ornithologist**.

I want to learn about **mammals**. You can be a **mammalogist**.

I want to learn about **all sorts of animals**. You can be a **zoologist**.

THIS IS A BORZOI BOOK PUBLISHED BY ALFRED A. KNOPF   Text copyright © 2016 by Jess Keating   Interior illustrations copyright © 2016 by David DeGrand
All rights reserved. Published in the United States by Alfred A. Knopf, an imprint of Random House Children's Books, a division of Penguin Random House LLC, New York.
Knopf, Borzoi Books, and the colophon are registered trademarks of Penguin Random House LLC.

Visit us on the Web! randomhousekids.com   Educators and librarians, for a variety of teaching tools, visit us at RHTeachersLibrarians.com

Library of Congress Cataloging-in-Publication Data
Keating, Jess, author. Pink is for blobfish : discovering the world's perfectly pink animals / by Jess Keating ; illustrations by David DeGrand. — First edition.
pages   cm.   Summary: An informative introduction to the weirdest, wildest, pinkest creatures in the animal kingdom.
ISBN 978-0-553-51227-4 (trade) — ISBN 978-0-553-51228-1 (lib. bdg.) — ISBN 978-0-553-51229-8 (ebook)
1. Animals—Color—Juvenile literature. 2. Pink—Juvenile literature. I. DeGrand, David, illustrator. II. Title.
QL767.K43 2016   591.47'2—dc23   2015013906

The illustrations in this book were created using ink and digital coloring.
MANUFACTURED IN MALAYSIA   February 2016   10 9 8 7 6 5 4 3 2 1   First Edition

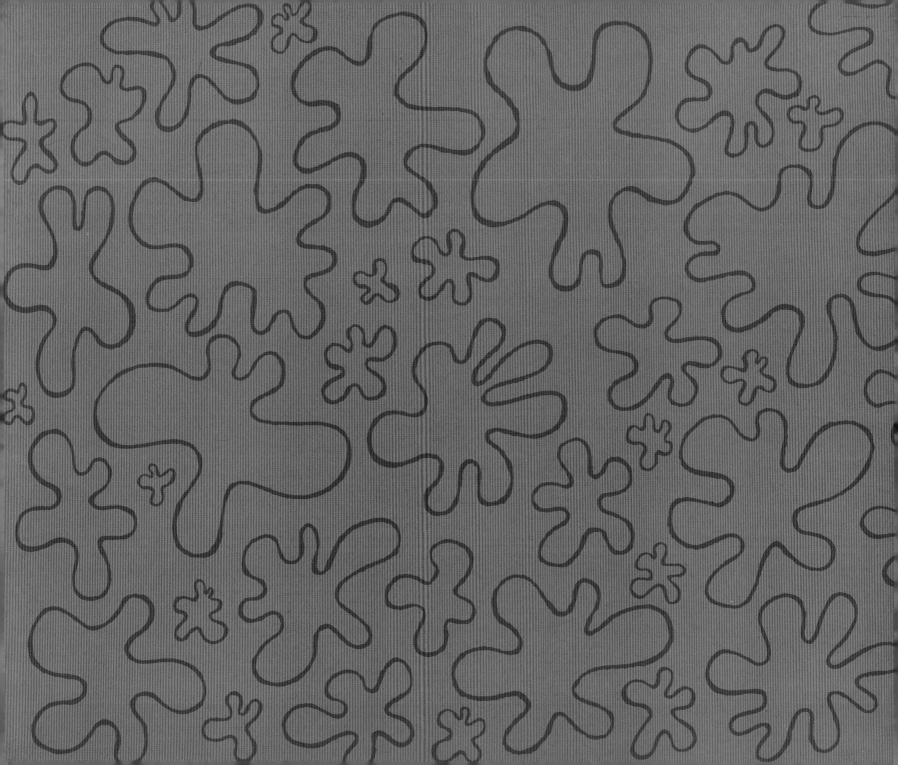